CASE DISMISSED

THE TIM TODD STORY

By Dr. Tim Todd

COPYRIGHT © 2012

Revival Fires® Ministries, Inc.

The Ministry of Dr. Tim Todd

505 Good Hope Road • West Monroe, Louisiana 71291

318.396.HOPE (4673) • www.revivalfires.org

Scripture quotations are taken from the
King James Version of the Bible.
Public Domain.

CASE DISMISSED

THE TIM TODD STORY

*Please Note: Some names in this book have been changed
to protect those who wish to remain anonymous.*

CASE DISMISSED

THE TIM TODD STORY

DEDICATED TO
my Dad, Cecil Todd
AND
my Mom, Barbara Todd

Like any child, there were plenty of times I rebelled against my parents. There were times I was sure they were wrong and I was right. And since I was called into the same vocation as my dad, I was often under a large shadow.

Over the years, I have preached revivals in churches all across America. Many times when I've been introduced to people, they have said things to me like "I gave my heart to the Lord in one of your dad's crusades." I remember a gentleman that got saved in one of my revivals who conveyed to me that his dad had given his heart to the Lord forty years prior in one of my dad's revivals.

It wasn't always easy being the son of Cecil Todd. I'm sure my son would tell you the same thing about me. Neither of us was perfect. We had our share of disagreements. But my mom and dad were Christian parents to our family in the very best sense of the term.

My parents saw to it that we were brought up in the training and instruction of the Lord. They taught me to be a child of my heavenly Father, as well as their child. My dad is my spiritual hero! He is the one who officiated my wedding. He is also the one who spanked me with the BIG WHITE BELT, although not as often as I deserved.

My parents grounded me, loved me, cared for me, and provided for me. But most of all, they brought me up in the training and instruction of the Lord. I will always have the greatest love and respect for my mom and dad and I dedicate this book to them.

> *Train up a child in the way he should go: and when he is old, he will not depart from it.* PROVERBS 22:6

---- ----

A Special Thanks

I also wish to thank Carolyn Wilde, author of numerous books, including, **We've Come This Far By Faith, Smitten Shepherds, Torchbearers,** and **A Tale of Two Cousins**, for her help in turning my life story into this book.

TABLE OF CONTENTS

STARING DEATH
IN THE FACE

Death from a massive overdose of cocaine is a
hideous sight. I know. I saw myself die.

I could not control my eyes. I felt them rolling back in my head.

I watched my body slump down into the vehicle.

I was no longer in my body, but above it.

I watched my wife beating on my convulsing form. I continued to
watch until my body grew still.

Time as I'd known it stopped. Everything went into slow motion.
There was an unearthly hush, yet every sound was amplified.

My wife looked terrified. Then her form blurred and faded, and I
was no longer staring down at my crumpled body.

I was looking in horror at two hideous creatures that had appeared
before me. I knew they had come to claim me.

My drug saturated body was out of their reach, but they had not come for my body. They had come for my soul.

Their sneers warped their deformed features.

They filled the air with a terrible smell.

I was helpless before them.

There was nothing I could say... nothing I could do. I knew, and they knew, that I belonged with them.

The hell my Dad had warned me about was real. So many times I heard his warnings.

"Don't wait until it is too late."

I had. Now Dad would be burying his own son, knowing he had waited — and it was too late. ***Poor Dad. Dad...***

DIVORCE

THE WORD THAT SHATTERED MY CHILDHOOD was one I thought I'd never hear him speak.

He called me into his office. When I left, I only heard one word drumming in my mind: ***Divorce.***

Dad and Mom's divorce didn't only shatter a home and divide a marriage that had endured for a quarter of a century, it also divided me from my childhood years of innocence. Does a parent realize what divorce does to his child?

My home had been my refuge from the world — my place of total security. I took it for granted.

Home was where my Dad and Mom were, always had been, and always would be — ***together.*** I took them for granted, too. I never looked at their marriage and thought "til death do us part", but I had believed that phrase applied to them. Death would be the only thing that could part my parents.

Home was the place where I would live, sleep, and eat until I grew up and left its comfort to begin life on my own. But when I heard the finality in Dad's voice when he spoke that one awful word, I knew that the home I had believed in was forever gone.

I guess it's something like air. I just expect that it will be available when I breathe. I never think about it. Only if it was no longer there would I think about the presence of air. Then a short time of gasping would replace my long time of breathing.

Or I could say it's like walking. I don't expect the ground to fall out from underneath me when I take my next step. But earthquakes happen. The ground disappears and people and buildings sink beneath it. Some are never found again.

That one seven-letter word instantly changed all I had believed in. Sure, it happened to lots of parents of kids I knew. But in my wildest imaginations, I never once thought that I would hear the word in my Christian home from my preacher Dad.

I didn't waste a second or a thought worrying about Mom or Dad. All I could think about was *me*. I suppose this is what all kids think about when their parents split. Who was I supposed to live with? Would they fight over me? Would either one want me in their new life?

Until that day, I had never once thought about where I would live. I would live with my Dad and Mom — wherever they were. They were my providers. Where they lived, I would live. Where they moved, I would move. Any home they lived in would include a room for me. Home was a place that would always be, and Dad and Mom were words that went together, never separately.

I guess I think of that *word* as the Great Divide. It not only divided my parents, but it carved a line across my life. It was something like B.C. and A.D.; the Southern and Northern Hemispheres; heaven and hell. My childhood stopped as I crossed the line into rebellion and confusion. I was sixteen years old.

There was a Bible verse that Dad used in his sermons. *"If the foundations be destroyed, what can the righteous do?"* PSALM 11:3

I guess he used it when he preached about America's fall from righteousness. But I could use that verse for me. "If the foundations be destroyed, what can a kid do?" Everything I believed in was destroyed.

It was then that I decided that Christianity apparently had no answers to life. Christianity couldn't even keep a marriage together.

I remembered hearing about the value of family. Value? *Divorce* made the word *family* meaningless. My descent into darkness began with the hearing of that word. I didn't just turn to the world to find answers for my life. I made a conscious decision to turn my back on God. All that I'd heard about Him having the answers hadn't worked in my family. I was angry. I couldn't fight the divorce.

By the time I learned about it, it was already settled. I decided to find someone to fight. School was a good place to start. A lot of kids were looking for fights there. What did it matter if I broke a nose or two and was suspended? Who cared? I was moving anyway. And I planned to take my anger with me.

HELD CAPTIVE BY DRUGS

IT WAS A BIGGER AND CLASSIER SCHOOL that was about to get a new student: a mad, cruel, and angry one.

"Wrath is cruel, and anger is outrageous ..." PROVERBS 27:4

I guess some would even consider me outrageous.

I had one big concern in this school. How was I supposed to fit in? I soon learned who the popular kids were. They were the ones drinking, smoking, and doing drugs. I'd listened to hours of preaching against these three "sins". The church crowd had described the kids who drank, smoked, and did drugs as "worldly."

They were perfect for the new "worldly" me. If alcohol and drugs were the world's answers to drown the pain of living, I was ready to see if they worked. Anything was better than Christianity.

I was drinking and smoking at a keg party when someone offered me a marijuana joint. The voices of those around me quieted to see how far I would go to be cool. I would go as far as I had to. If it meant doing drugs, give them to me.

I loved the party life. If this was the evil world - count me in! For the first time, I was no longer watching the "in" crowd. I was in it!

Alcohol and marijuana were the door that led me in.

They were also the door that led me out! I walked out of my old life of "Christianity." I had finally found a way to deal with my parents and my anger. I had something good to live for at last — ***drugs!***

I wonder how my highly respected Dad who preached on national television would feel about my new life? Not that I cared. Why would I care about his reputation? Nobody consulted me before splitting the home. I would consult no one about the way I chose to live.

Dad made the mistake of trusting me. He continued to go on his missionary trips and evangelistic meetings and leave me at the house by myself. As soon as his car would leave the driveway, I'd turn the music up, invite my new friends over, and we would load the house and ourselves up with alcohol and drugs. I'd check Dad's calendar and remove the evidence before he'd get back home from trying to save the world. I would randomly drop the trash at neighbor's houses on my way to school.

One day after his preaching trip and my big party, I breezed into Dad's office and found him sitting at his desk.

I stared around him. His office was piled high with the trash I had dumped: beer cans, cigarette butts, marijuana paraphernalia ... and stationary with Cecil Todd's name on it. The neighbor's German Shepherd had gone through the trash bags I threw in his front yard on my way to school. When the neighbor, a highway patrolman, found our trash littering his front yard, he gathered it all up and delivered it to Dad.

"Welcome Home, Dad."

Maybe that was the day my Dad realized his son was a lost soul who needed saving.

Nothing changed. I just got smarter. I learned that burned toast was stronger than the smell of cigarettes and marijuana. Dad would walk in the door and say, "Tim, the house looks great! But why does it always smell like burnt toast in here?"

When he was in town, I had to go to church with him. I used bottles of mouthwash and cologne to hide the smell of marijuana. Visine got the red out of my eyes. I'd sit in church with the worshipers.

I was a worshiper, too, I thought smugly. My gods were sex, drugs, and rock and roll.

I was still reeling from the divorce announcement when I was slammed with another announcement. Dad had met Linda a short time after the divorce. They dated a few times and announced their wedding. My brother, Jon, was supposed to be Dad's best man. He flew to where the wedding would be held in Linda's home church but never even left the airport. Someone else would have to stand with Dad. He got right back on the airplane and returned home.

I got drunk and high on the trip from Joplin to Leavenworth to attend the wedding. When Dad realized that Jon wasn't coming, he asked me to be his best man.

I made it through the wedding, but I didn't do so well when I
got back home. A new wife had replaced Mom. Her teenage son,
Chuck, was calling my Dad his Dad even before they were married.
I couldn't figure out how I was supposed to fit into this new family.
I wasn't ready to see my Dad with another wife. I hadn't even had
time to get used to home without Mom.

I managed to graduate somehow. What a relief to be independent
from Dad! Acting the part of an obedient son was getting more
difficult by the day. The life he wanted for me and the lifestyle I had
decided to live were extreme opposites. Do you think I cried about
leaving "home"? I felt only relief. I would no longer have to hide
evidence of my parties - at least from him. I would now have to hide
my habits and partying from the administrators of a Bible college!

Dad required all of us kids to attend Bible college for one year when
we graduated from high school. I was in no spiritual condition
to attend a Bible college. I tried not to think of where I was
going. Instead I concentrated on what and who I was leaving. On
graduation day I packed my Dodge Magnum so I could leave the
next morning.

When I arrived at Dallas Christian College, the administrators were
excited to meet Cecil Todd's son.

"This is great," they said. "We have a perfect roommate for you. He
is a severely troubled, suicidal student. You will be able to minister
to him!"

They didn't know that I was the last person that should be rooming
with a student who was emotionally unstable. Being Cecil Todd's
son did not make me God's son!

My roommate went home during spring break. I had no place I wanted to go, but there was plenty I planned to do! I had found other students at college who liked to party. I invited them all to my dorm room for a good time of drinking.

I was not in the dorm room when my roommate arrived back a day earlier than I expected. He walked into our room that was still littered with beer bottles, beer cans, marijuana leftovers, and cigarette butts.

He turned me into the very unhappy administration. They kicked me out of the dorm but did not expel me from school.

I was determined to finish the remaining six weeks of the semester, because the alternative was moving back in with Dad, Linda, and Dad's new son.

Since I couldn't afford to rent an apartment or stay in a motel, I turned my car into my new home. Each night I would find a back alley or parking lot and go to sleep. On the way to school each morning I would stop at the closest gas station that had a restroom with an outside entrance. I'd wash my hair and face in the usually grimy sink. On the weekends I would go to my brother Jon's apartment in Arlington where I could take a shower.

I finished the first semester of Bible college. Then a financially lucrative opportunity became available, and I began importing and selling Mercedes sports cars from Germany. Money poured into my hands - and right back out. I had not only graduated from high school, but had graduated from marijuana and alcohol and entered the surreal world of cocaine.

I left Dallas and moved to Tulsa, Oklahoma. I soon met and married Ann, one of Tulsa's top drug dealers. We had only one thing in common: our love for drugs.

Dad came to our wedding. It only took a glance at him to realize he brought along his broken heart.

I knew exactly what he was praying: "God, do whatever it takes to get Tim right with You."

I didn't care. I had no faith in God, so why would I fear my Dad's prayers to a God I didn't believe in?

Whatever it takes...

Neither one of us knew then the hell that I would descend into before I looked up into the face of God, took His hand, and let Him lift me up from the cesspool my life had become.

It's funny about cocaine. The highs were getting shorter. They would begin good. Then, even before they would completely fade, I would be left with a desperate craving for my next one.

I hadn't slept in three days. I was enjoying a cocaine binge. Actually, maybe enjoying is not the word I should use. I was in the car when finally, out of sheer desperation, I injected a huge dose of cocaine into my veins.

I learned that day that it takes just one last injection to overdose. I'd seen movies of people's eyes rolling back in their sockets. That was the day I experienced it. I had no control over my eyes. I could literally feel them moving upward. That was the day I died. That was the day I looked down at my convulsing body until it stilled. That was the day I came face to face with demons who did not belong on earth but in hell. That was the day I wasn't sure the world held the answers to life after all.

Was it the prayers of those who still had hope for me that turned the demons back from their mission that awful day?

IGNORING THE VOICE OF GOD

I HEARD A VOICE SPEAKING in what seemed to be a vacuum of a silence that could be felt.

"Young man, you were a goner. Somebody upstairs must really be watching out for you."

I didn't know where I was. The last thing I remembered was being above my body at the mercy of demonic creatures. I finally realized I was in the back of an ambulance.

It was the paramedic who had revived me who was speaking. I didn't attempt to answer him.

Another voice spoke. I knew immediately who it was. The Holy Spirit didn't speak into my ears but into my heart. He said, "Tim, either you turn to God or you will be turned into an everlasting hell."

I ignored both voices. No one "upstairs" cared enough about me to watch out for me. Where was "God" when my parents split? And as for "turning to God," what good would that do? God would take one look at me and turn away from me! I'd gone too far. I'd done too much. I'd overdosed on sin.

I stoked my furnace of boiling anger and turned back to my drugs.

It didn't take long to find out that the world had no answers for troubled marriages either. Now it was my marriage that was in trouble. Actually, I was too drugged to realize it until it was almost too late.

It was a shock to learn that Ann wanted me out of her life. Divorce, however, was not the solution for her getting rid of me. She decided on murder.

A MESSAGE
OF LOVE

A friend and I decided to put together a concert for Tulsa headlining what was then a nationally popular hard rock band, "Head East." People don't go to rock concerts just to hear music. They go to party, and they expect plenty of drugs to be available.

There are usually one or two people who are responsible for supplying all the drugs for each concert. Ann was the supplier for this one.

I don't know how, but Dad found out about the concert. He sent his friend who sang in his revival crusades to find me.

He was supposed to give me a four word message from Dad: "I love you, Tim."

He never did find me in the crowd. He finally gave up and left Dad's message with one of the security guards.

It didn't make me happy. I didn't need to be reminded that I was running from both Dad and God. What I didn't know is that I was running straight into Danger with a capital D.

THE MURDER PLOT

HER NAME WAS DEBRA, AND SHE WAS ANN'S FRIEND. Debra befriended Ann for a reason. Ann had drugs and Debra was a thief. The friendship was very profitable for Debra, as she and her husband, Robert, had been stealing drugs from Ann for a long time. I told Ann that they were stealing from her, but she didn't believe me.

Ann trusted Debra. Debra despised me. She knew that I knew what she and Robert were doing.

Debra convinced Ann that they needed to get rid of me permanently. Their plan to murder me almost worked. We were at a party when I started to lose total control of my body and mind. Just before I completely lost my faculties, I noticed white powder floating in the bottom of one of my drinks. Then I noticed Debra looking intently at me. Her lips curled with a sadistic grin.

"What is this?" I asked her.

She knew I was going to die. She had nothing to hide. Corpses don't talk. She was gloating as she answered, "Tim, there are enough Quaaludes inside of you now to kill a horse."

I learned later that Debra and Ann had plotted together to incapacitate me with the mixture of drugs and alcohol. Then they planned to dump me in a section of Tulsa where crime was ignored. They had already paid two thugs to get rid of my body. If I was somehow still alive, they had been ordered to kill me.

I was slipping fast. My mind was whirling and my body was growing numb. I had just enough sense to know that I had to get away from Ann and Debra. As I stumbled to my car, my mind played and replayed two thoughts like a broken record: "I am dying. I am on my way to hell."

I somehow got behind the wheel of my car, but I was in no condition to drive. I crashed the car into a curb. I crawled out of the car and inched my way out of the street. I finally collapsed behind the brick entrance of a housing addition. I was told later that I remained there in an unconscious stupor for several hours.

Then God, in His mercy...
   God, in His love...
      God, in His amazing grace...

sent two policemen to the scene of the accident. It was while searching for the driver of the crashed car that they found me.

I was rushed to the hospital. When I regained consciousness, one of the policemen who had found me was now guarding me. He greeted me back to the land of the living with these words: "Young man, it is a miracle that you are alive. The doctors say you should be dead from all the drugs and alcohol in you. As soon as you are released, you are going straight to the slammer."

I didn't respond.

I finally got my chance to escape when he walked to the nurse's station to flirt with a nurse. I unhooked my IV, left the hospital and hitchhiked a ride home.

Home?

Once again, home was not a place of security and comfort. The first thing I saw when I walked in the door was the shock on Ann's face. She managed to mask it quickly with a look of concern. Somehow she even managed to get tears to run down her face.

"Tim! It wasn't my fault! I didn't know what I was doing. I was so confused. It wasn't my idea to kill you. Please forgive me!"

I wasn't in the mood for forgiveness. My own wife had just conspired with her friend to knock me off. Her attempted murder managed to break down the trust barrier just a little bit!

Did I stay with her? Of course I did! She was my only source of drugs. And drugs were my life!

Unfortunately, Ann and I had not heard the last of Debra.

DEBRA—AGAIN

I COULD NOT BELIEVE DEBRA HAD THE AUDACITY to call me after trying to kill me! What is even more unbelievable now is that I was stupid enough to listen to her. The lust for drugs and money to buy them override all sense and judgment.

"I want to make it up to you, Tim," she said in her silky voice. "We have someone who is ready to pay $10,000 for drugs right now. If you will provide them, we will let you have all the profit."

Ann and I greedily agreed.

We got the drugs from our supplier on credit, bagged them up, and delivered them to the address Debra had provided.

It was Debra who called from the front door, "The buyers are hiding in the back room. They don't want you to know who they are. I'll take the drugs to them. They insist on trying them before they buy them."

We got as far as the foyer when she grabbed the bag of drugs. We learned later that Debra and her husband, Robert, climbed out the back window and fled with the drugs.

We were still waiting for her in the foyer when Ann's ex-boyfriend, Scott, walked into the room. He put a gun to my head and said, "If I can't have Ann, nobody can."

I heard two things simultaneously: the cock of his pistol and a knock at the front door.

A man's head appeared in the partially opened door.

"Is anybody here?"

I answered, "Yes, we're here! Come on in!"

As he walked in, I saw Scott hide his gun.

It was the next door neighbor who said, "I noticed people climbing out of the back window and came over to see if everything is okay."

I answered, "Everything is fine here. Please excuse us. We are late for an appointment."

An appointment...

I grabbed Ann's hand and we rushed out the door.

Once again, God had saved me from an appointment with death.

Now I had another major problem.

I had lost the drugs. I didn't have $10,000 to pay the drug supplier.

I knew him well enough to know that he would think nothing of killing me. I would become his message to other dealers: pay up or die.

I was given the ultimatum I expected.

"You have one week. Produce the drugs or the money, or pay with your life."

ARRESTED

WE NEEDED TO FIND DEBRA AND ROBERT AND RECOVER the drugs they had stolen from us. We hired a private investigator. He did his work well and told us where they were hiding.

This time we were ready for them. We loaded our guns and broke into their house. We frantically searched, but couldn't find either the money or the drugs. We had to get $10,000 somehow. We decided to steal everything of value in their house to raise the money we needed.

We had no idea that they had seen us coming. Debra, the thief, dared to call the police to report a burglary in progress! Then she and Robert hid behind their house.

When we came out carrying stolen goods, they began shooting at us! They held us at gunpoint until the police arrived. We were the ones arrested for armed burglary!

We breathed a sigh of relief when we made bail. ***Freedom.***

Our relief lasted only until we walked out the door of the police department. The drug supplier was waiting for us and he was not happy. Again we were staring death in the face.

For some unknown reason, he spared our lives. Then he put the word out that no one in Tulsa was to provide drugs for us.

If there were no drugs available to us in Tulsa, our only choice was to move. Drugs were our life—our air—our food.

Ann and I took a long look at each other. What we saw brought no pleasure to either one of us. Our marriage had never been based on love. If we couldn't use each other to feed our drug habit, what use did either one of us have for the other?

Ann and her brother, Don, made the decision that we would move where they could sell drugs. We loaded most of our belongings into a U-Haul truck. Since they wouldn't all fit in one load, Ann said, "Tim, you stay here with the rest of the things, and Don and I will take the first load. We'll unload our things and then come right back to get the rest."

I waited... *and waited.*

When would I quit believing people? How could I have been so foolish as to believe the woman who had tried to murder me would come back for me?

I lost everything I owned. I sat on the floor of the house that had just been emptied of everything of value. I looked at the trash that littered the floor around me.

Then I looked at my life and saw another heap of trash.

I thought for a long time before deciding on the only solution to life: end it.

I picked up my .45 and loaded it.

This wasn't the first time I had stared death in the face. This time I would keep my appointment and get it over with.

I had heard my Dad preach that the wages of sin is death. He was right. At twenty-one years of age, I had nothing or no one left to live for. Payday had come for me.

I wondered how my life had come to this. I dared to look at my past.

I saw a parade of my sins passing before me. Anger came first; lies followed; then the casual sex, cigarettes, drinking, marijuana, cocaine, and other drugs. The parade passed out of sight and I sat empty, alone.

Even Ann was gone. I didn't miss her. But I desperately missed what she had to offer me—a ready supply of drugs.

I didn't recognize the voice then, but I know now who it was. The devil began to encourage me to quit thinking and shoot.

"You will be better off dead. Your family will be happier when you kill yourself. They won't have to keep praying for you. You are an embarrassment to your Dad's ministry. He will be relieved when you're dead. Do the right thing for once in your life. Quit stalling. Shoot."

I thought about the choices I'd made.

> I'd chosen lies over the Lord.
> I'd chosen cigarettes over the Savior.
> I'd chosen cocaine over Christ.
> I'd chosen money over the Master.
> I'd chosen marijuana over the Messiah.

Now it was time to choose the gun over God.

As I lifted the gun up under my chin, I said, "Lord, if You're listening to me, I need Your help."

When I said *"Help,"* the telephone rang.

I picked it up and heard Mom. She was calling from Joplin, Missouri.

"Tim, I was praying for you. I had to call you right now. Are you okay?"

I lowered the gun and said without thinking, "Mom, I want to come home."

The God I didn't believe in had answered my prayer for help. I decided to return the favor and straighten my life out. When I got myself good enough, quit drugs, and cleaned up my act, I would present myself to God.

I went to Joplin. The bars were open and the drug scene was waiting for me. Life in Joplin was good!

GOD'S LIFELINE

IT WAS ONE OF MY TYPICAL SATURDAY NIGHTS. I and one of my friends were where we always were on Saturday nights. Mark and I were in a bar and we were both slap drunk. Mark came up with the crazy idea that totally changed my life.

"Tim, it's Saturday night. Tomorrow is Sunday. Let's go to church in the morning."

I looked at him. He definitely didn't look like or smell like a Christian. If he had been a Christian, I would have laughed in his face.

Since he was as drunk as I was, I answered, "Sure, Mark! Why not?"

We walked into *Lifeline Full Gospel Church* reeking of tobacco, marijuana, and alcohol. I knew what would happen. The people inside would scatter to the four walls when they saw us.

I was wrong. They greeted us warmly with handshakes and hugs. I looked around the church in shock. Somehow I knew that I had walked into a church full of genuine Christians. Their smiles were real. They were lit up from the inside out.

Then they began to praise and worship the Lord.

Something deep inside me wanted to join them.

I knew all about church services and I knew what sinners were supposed to do in church. After all, I was the preacher's kid!

Now I was the sinner who finally realized I desperately needed— and wanted—a Savior.

I was supposed to wait for the preacher to preach his sermon and call sinners to the front of the church. Not until then was I supposed to walk quietly to the front of the church, kneel at the altar, and pray.

The trouble was, I didn't want to wait to talk to God. I needed Him, and I needed Him now! What else mattered? When I needed to talk to my Dad at his office, I didn't have to make an appointment and go through the receptionist, secretary, and his personal assistant like everyone else did. I just walked boldly through the side door that led directly into his office and started talking! He didn't rebuke me. He welcomed me! He was my Dad! I was his son!

Couldn't I just do the same thing here?

Yes! I could—and I would!

The congregation was only halfway through with their praise service when I jumped up and ran down the aisle as fast as I could. My knees hit the floor in front of that altar and something broke inside me.

This time I knew I couldn't clean myself up. I couldn't remove the bitterness and anger anymore than I could remove my own appendix. I needed major surgery. I didn't need another temporary first aid bandage to keep the poison from spreading through me and pouring out of me. I needed a permanent cure. I was about to drown in sin and I needed the only One who could pull me out.

> **"Help me, Lord! I am Tim—not the preacher's kid, but the sinner ..."**

It was *my* heart that had turned black with anger and bitterness when my parents divorced. I could have helped them through that terrible time in their lives. Instead, I added hurt and heartache to the two people who loved me more than anyone else in the world.

How could I have blamed them for my sins? Dad and Mom weren't the ones destroying themselves with drugs, robbing homes, and holding guns to their heads.

I had been blinded! The problem was never with Dad and Mom. Mom was the one who had stopped me from killing myself by her telephone call. She continued to love and serve the Lord in Branson, Missouri, and has never remarried. Dad was still faithfully preaching. I was the one who reacted to a sad situation by abandoning my heart to hatred and my life to sin.

My only hope was God's amazing grace.

I stayed on my knees until I *knew* I had met Jesus Christ. I prayed until I *knew* that He had come into my heart. I waited until I *knew* that He saved my soul from sin, death, and destruction. I didn't rise to my feet until I *knew* that Jesus lived inside me!

When He came inside, He began the process immediately of changing me from the inside out!

I had craved sin. Now I craved His Word. I found life in the Bible!

I no longer hung out at the bars. I hung out with God's people at church! The Lifeline Full Gospel Church was well named. It became a lifeline for me. Missionary Don Jones and his wife, Pastor Mary Lou Jones, were there to help me take my first few faltering steps as I began my new walk in Christ.

I always had to be surrounded with drinkers and guys doing drugs. Now I loved just spending time with Jesus.

I couldn't wait to tell Ann that I was a changed man! I was about to learn that she had no intention of becoming a changed woman.

CASE DISMISSED. FORGIVEN!

I TRIED TO CALL ANN, BUT SHE REFUSED to return my calls. It was all right. I could wait a little while longer. I would see her in Tulsa, where we both had to appear in court to face armed burglary charges.

My attorney told me to come to the court house prepared to do time because of the severity of the charges against me.

I was prepared, mentally, physically, and spiritually. I would not be alone. I was a free man no matter what the judge ruled. The Son of God Himself had set me free from my sins. I had a promise from the Bible: *"If the Son therefore shall make you free, ye shall be free indeed."* JOHN 8:36

No prison cell could take my freedom from me.

I found Ann in the front area of the courthouse. I excitedly told her what Jesus had done for me.

"I'm free, Ann! Jesus has saved me! I am free from cocaine, alcohol, cigarettes, anger, bitterness, marijuana, the sex, stealing! Jesus can set you free, too!"

She looked at me and said, "No, Tim. He can't."

"Yes, Ann, He can! I thought the same thing you are thinking! I thought I had gone too far away from Him and fell too deep into sin. But Jesus saved me, Ann! And He can save you, too!"

Her next words broke my heart.

"No, Tim, you don't understand what I am saying. God can't save me because I love my sin too much."

She turned her back on me and walked into the court room.

It was hard to concentrate on the trial. I had been so sure that Ann would want to begin a new life with Jesus. I dreamed of a beautiful marriage based on love instead of drugs. I had planned to convince her to ask God to save her, pray with her, and then to leave the courthouse together, hand in hand.

Now I had to face the truth. Ann wanted nothing to do with the Savior who had given me a new life. I knew Ann, and I had no doubt her words were final.

The preliminaries of the trial were over. Our case was given to the judge. He called for the people whose house we had robbed. When no one responded, the frustrated judge called for the attorneys from both sides to meet in his chambers. They returned in about five minutes.

The judge sat down, picked up his gavel, and looked at me... and smiled! Then he slammed the gavel down and spoke two unbelievable words: ***"Case dismissed."***

I went into the courtroom a free man.

And I walked out of the courtroom a free man.

I felt God pouring His love into me.

"Tim, this is what I did for you. I saw all your sins, but I slammed the gavel down and announced in heaven, *"Case dismissed. Forgiven."*

Was I guilty? Yes.

Did God demand justice? Yes.

Then Jesus went to the cross and paid the price.

He died instead of me. His blood was shed instead of mine.

And my sentence was served by the only One who walked this earth and never sinned.

"Paid in full. Case dismissed."

What a range of emotions had filled me that day.

Excitement, believing Ann would receive Jesus into her life.

Crushing disappointment when she walked away from Jesus and from me.

Uncertainty about what my future would hold when the judge ruled.

Relief when all charges against me were dropped.

Love when the Lord drew near and assured me again of His love and forgiveness.

God had one more message for me before I left the courtroom foyer. It was the most shocking one of all.

MADE USABLE

- -

"Tim, if you will allow me to make you usable, I will use you in these last days."

I knew His voice, but I couldn't believe His message.

How could God use me? I was still in awe that He had loved me enough to save me. But *use me* to serve Him?

"God, there is no way You can use me. I have fallen into the depths of sin. My life has been trashed."

Yet I knew He meant what He said. Making winners out of sinners and scrappers out of scraps was God's specialty.

He had done this time after time. The Bible is full of stories of His mercy. I was the preacher's kid!

I knew about Rahab, the high class prostitute of the Old Testament. God slammed the gavel down and announced in heaven: *"Case dismissed. Forgiven."* God *used* her to become one of the long line of people who descended from Adam and brought Jesus, God's only begotten Son, into the world.

I knew about the woman Jesus met at the well. We aren't told her name, but we are told about her past. When she met Jesus, she had already been married to five husbands and was living with another man. God slammed the gavel down and announced in heaven, *"Case dismissed. Forgiven."* God then *used* her to bring the men of her city to Jesus.

There was the woman caught in the act of adultery. The religious leaders of her day dragged her to Jesus to be judged, condemned, and stoned. He looked through her eyes, into her heart, and said: "Neither do I condemn thee: go, and sin no more." And once again the gavel was slammed down in heaven, and God announced, *"Case dismissed. Forgiven."* Jesus *used* her as an example of His amazing grace.

There was the maniac from Gadara. He was filled with thousands of demons. It took just one meeting with Jesus to set him free. God slammed the gavel down and announced in heaven, *"Case dismissed. Forgiven."* God *used* him to become an evangelist in Decapolis - a region in Syria of ten cities!

There was the thief, condemned to crucifixion for his life of sin. He was hours, perhaps only moments, from death when he realized that he was dying next to the sinless Lord who had come from heaven to save sinners. It took just one nine word prayer to alter his destiny: "Lord, remember me when thou comest into thy kingdom." The answer Jesus gave him gives hope to every sinner: "Verily I say unto thee, To day shalt thou be with me in paradise." God's gavel again came down in heaven. Can you hear the joy in His voice as He cried, *"Case dismissed! Forgiven!"* We tell and retell his story today. God *used* that thief to paint a picture of His love for sinners.

Saul was an angry man with a mission. He literally breathed out threats to Christians who dared to follow Christ. He condemned them to prisons and took pleasure in their slaughter. He was on his way to Damascus to arrest more of them when Jesus spoke to him from the sky. Blinded by the Light and humbled by the words of the One he dared to hate, he stumbled into Damascus, his life forever changed by that one short encounter. God again slammed the gavel down and announced in heaven: *"Case dismissed. Forgiven."*

God changed Saul's name to Paul and *used* him to write over half of the New Testament!

> *"Tim, if you would allow me to make you usable,*
> *I will use you in these last days."*

I was ashamed now of my hasty and foolish response: "God, there is no way you can use me. I have fallen into the depths of sin. My life has been trashed."

Every single one of the people the Lord had brought to my mind could have made the same excuse. Yet they made themselves "usable" and offered what remained of their lives to the One who set them free from their sins. And He used each of them.

I would allow God to make me usable.

I still had one more court date ahead. This time I was on the prosecution side. I was trying to retrieve my possessions that Ann's brother had stolen from me. I was about to receive the most shocking news of my life—and of my wife.

ANN

I TOLD MY SIDE OF THE STORY TO THE JUDGE. He then called Don to the stand to give his testimony.

I looked over at my brother-in-law and was stunned at what I saw. His face was ashen and he was literally trembling.

The color left my face and I began to tremble too when I heard his stumbling words.

"Your Honor, Tim's wife, Ann... my sister... Ann... died suddenly. It happened three days ago. There was an aneurism on her brain. Her funeral is this afternoon."

The judge looked at me.

I was shocked. It was all I could do to say the words that the court demanded to end the case: "Your Honor, I drop the charges."

The judge picked up the gavel, slammed it down, and announced, "Case dismissed."

Ann's judgment would come in a higher court.

The gavel would be slammed down, but the beautiful word "Forgiven" would not follow her judgment.

The last words Ann spoke to me replayed themselves over and over in my mind.

"God can't save me because I love my sin too much."

Ann had put into words what most people speak only with their lifestyle. *"God can't save me because I love my sin too much..."*

Ann didn't know then how soon her appointment with death would be kept.

> *"It is appointed unto men once to die, but after this the judgment. He that is unjust, let him be unjust still: and he which is filthy, let him be filthy still: and he that is righteous, let him be righteous still: and he that is holy, let him be holy still."*
> HEBREWS 9:27 AND REVELATION 22:11

Ann chose to stand before God unforgiven, unjust, and filthy.

She could have stood before Him forgiven, righteous, and clean.

"I love my sin too much. I love my sin..."

She now had neither sin nor a Savior. Both were forever out of her reach.

THE WONDERS
OF MY SAVIOR

I NO LONGER WAS JUST A HEARER OF THE MESSAGE that the wages of sin is death. Now I knew it by experience. I knew that sin was only a temporary high. When the fun was over, all that was left was an empty heart, an aching head, a tormented mind, and death—death to friendships; death to marriages; death to bodies; death to souls.

With an undeniable call of God into the ministry, I would spend the rest of my life telling anyone who would listen to me about the awfulness of sin and the wonders of my Savior.

Sin's tragic results are seen all through the Bible.

They had been just Bible stories that I had learned as a kid before. Now as I was reading them, I could feel the raw grief of people who have experienced sin's destruction.

I could see Adam and Eve as they were evicted from their beautiful home and the fellowship with their Creator. I could hear their sobs as they buried their murdered son and watched as their other son, the killer, walked out of their lives.

I could hear the terrified screams of the drowning multitudes who refused to listen to Noah, a preacher of righteousness.

I could feel the searing flames that spread through the cities of Sodom and Gomorrah, leaving only death and ashes in their wake.

I could see the agony of King Saul's heart reflected on his face as he committed his final act—suicide.

I could see the tears as David and Bathsheba buried their baby boy born of their sin of adultery.

I could hear Judas' last tortured cry as he hanged himself after betraying the Son of God.

The most heart-rending cry in all the Bible was the one that came from the Savior's mutilated body nailed to Calvary's cross. The weight of the sins of the entire world were crushing the life out of His sinless body. He felt their awful wages as His beloved Father turned away from Him. *"My God! My God! Why hast Thou forsaken me?"*

I did not love my sins too much. I laid them all at my Savior's feet. I wanted only deliverance from their hold on me, forgiveness for what I had become, and cleansing so I could be used. I had finally learned to despise my sins that had caused my precious Savior's death.

Through it all, He kept loving me. He was the only One with a remedy for sin.

"Come now, and let us reason together, saith the Lord: *though your sins be as scarlet, they shall be as white as snow ..."* ISAIAH 1:18

I learned by experience what it meant to have my Savior turn my black sins as white as snow.

When I finally knelt at His feet, He turned
My death into life,
My darkness into light,
My fear into faith,
My captivity into deliverance,
My rebellion into submission,
My lust into purity,
My hatred into love,
My covetousness into contentment,
My grudges into forgiveness,
My temper into gentleness,
My impatience into longsuffering,
My pride into meekness,
My lies into truth,
My curses into praise,
My complaints into thanksgiving,
My evil into righteousness, and
My sorrow into joy.

Ann loved her sin too much to turn to the only One who could save her soul.

I love my Savior too much to even think about turning back to my miserable life of sin.

It was when Jesus was dining in the home of a Pharisee that a woman with a reputation of a sinner knelt weeping at His feet, washed His feet with her tears, dried them with her hair, kissed them, and then anointed them with ointment.

Simon, the host, was shocked, thinking that Jesus did not realize who and what she was. He did not rebuke Jesus openly, but Jesus knew what he was thinking and answered his thoughts. Can you hear the sternness in His voice and see the disappointment in His eyes as Jesus reminded Simon that he had not provided water for His feet, greeted Him with a kiss, or anointed His head with oil?

And can you see His gentle eyes as He turned toward the woman and said, "Her sins, which are many, are forgiven; for she loved much: but to whom little is forgiven, the same loveth little."

How could I help but love my Savior? He has shown me mercy time and time again. He has forgiven me for every single one of my many sins.

The words the Lord spoke to me as I left the courtroom did not leave my mind. "Tim, if you would allow me to make you usable, I will use you in these last days."

I had heard one Bible verse many times from Dad's sermons:

> *"Therefore if any man be in Christ, he is a new*
> *creature: old things are passed away; behold, all*
> *things are become new."*
> II Corinthians 5:17

I felt as if I'd already lived a lifetime, yet I was only 22 years old. Old things had swiftly passed away. My marriage had died. My wife had died. My life as I'd lived it up until now was over. But what was ahead? How would God make all things new? Could He really use me in some way?

I wanted to serve my Lord with all my mind, soul, heart, and strength. There was one thing I could do. I could tell people about my Savior who loved me, died for me, forgave me, and saved me.

I soon learned firsthand that Jesus has not changed. I will tell you a few of the ways He has used me before I tell you that I learned by experience that my Savior is still a Miracle-Worker!

EVERYONE NEEDS JESUS!

SOME MAY QUESTION HOW JESUS COULD USE ME. There is only one way. My Lord slammed the gavel down in heaven and announced, *"Case Dismissed."* When He spoke those two words in heaven, I was set free on earth—free to spend the rest of my life serving Jesus with all my heart, soul, mind, and strength!

I have preached the gospel around the world, conducting evangelistic crusades in Africa, Russia, Latvia, India, Haiti, Mexico, the Bahamas, and the Middle East.

Tim conducting an evangelistic crusade in Combatoire, India. Over 100,000 attended and over 30,000 accepted Jesus Christ as their Savior.

Tim praying for Louisiana Governor, Bobby Jindal,
at the Governor's Mansion

I have preached in some of the largest churches in America and some of the worst slums in third world countries. I have preached to national political leaders and people who have nothing. They all have one thing in common: *every single one of them needs Jesus.*

I stood with my Dad, Dr. Tim LaHaye, Dr. James E. (Johnny) Johnson, Dr. Joseph Scheidler, and many other prominent leaders, delivering one million petitions voicing opposition to the continued killing of unborn babies through abortion. I spoke before the United States Supreme Court and the National Press Corporation.

Tim delivering over 1,000,000 signatures to restore voluntary Bible reading and prayer in schools.

I delivered over one million signatures of people who wanted the restoration of voluntary school prayer and Bible reading to the United States Congress, commanding the attention of then United States House Speaker Newt Gingrich, Congressman J. C. Watts, Senator Jesse Helms, Congressman Ernest Istook, and many other high ranking government officials.

I launched a national campaign to distribute the book that I had designed and published, *The Truth For Youth*, to every teenager in the United States. My goal was to bring teens face-to-face with the Gospel of Jesus Christ. I wanted to bring them a message of hope that would counter the ill effect of the liberal agenda aggressively being promoted to them in our public schools.

The Truth for Youth has been enthusiastically endorsed by Michael Reagan, Bishop T. D. Jakes, Pastor Rod Parsley, Pastor Steve Hill, Pastor Denny Duron, Actor Dean Jones, Pat Boone, the late Pastor Billy Joe Daugherty, the late Dr. Jerry Falwell, the late Dr. Bill Bright, the late Art Linkletter, and many other prominent Christian leaders.

Packed in its pages is the entire New Testament and powerful full color comic stories that teach absolute truths regarding issues facing our young people today: Sexual Purity, Sorcery and Witchcraft, Drug Addiction, Drunkenness, Peer Pressure, Pornography,

Homosexuality, Abortion, School Violence, Secular Rock Music, and more. Jesus' invitation to come to Him for salvation is incorporated into each story.

Over 1.5 million copies have already been distributed by teenagers who give the Bibles to their unsaved friends in school. I used the back cover of *The Truth For Youth* to display the students' legal rights to distribute Bibles on public school campuses during noninstructional time. I have received thousands of decision coupons from young people who have testified that they gave their hearts and lives to Jesus Christ.

One bold young lady gave *The Truth For Youth* to a gang leader and the entire gang turned to Jesus!

JOHN 8:32 says: *"And ye shall know the truth, and the truth shall make you free!"*

Only *Truth* breaks the chains of sin! Jesus said, *"I am the way, the truth, and the life: no man cometh unto the Father, but by me."* JOHN 14:6

There are nearly fifty-four million students in America's public schools. Forty million of them still do not have a Bible. Getting one into their hands is my top priority!

My Dad and I were asked by Russia's Minister of Education to provide Bibles as textbooks for Russia's public schools in September of 1991. We met in the Education Building in Moscow with Vladimir Saprykin, the Vice President of the Ministry of Education. He enthusiastically gave his approval!

Tim Todd distributing Bibles to Russian public school students.

Then he asked me a troubling question.

"What kind of Bible distribution program does America have for your public schools?"

Tim Todd distributing Bibles to Russian Red Army soldiers.

I was ashamed of my answer, but replied, "Russia has put God in school, but America has kicked Him out."

I have since helped **Revival Fires® International** distribute over two million Bibles to young people in Russia's public schools.

Revival Fires® was granted access to Russian military bases. We conducted "Russian Red Army Revival" services and distributed Bibles to the soldiers. Thousands of soldiers and officers are giving their lives to Jesus Christ! Over one million Bibles have already been distributed to the 2.5 million Russian soldiers.

GOD'S HEALING TOUCH

OFTEN WHEN I AM HOLDING EVANGELISTIC MEETINGS in churches, people ask me to pray for their healing.

I laid hands on a board member's wife at a church in Arkansas. She had a huge cancerous tumor mass on her kidney and was scheduled for surgery. The day after I prayed for her, she had another MRI. The doctor called her with these words: "I don't understand. The cancer was there. It is completely gone."

I don't know how the Lord takes the same hands that have stolen, taken drugs, and hurt people and uses them as a conduit for His healing power. I only know that He has said that believers would "lay hands on the sick, and they shall recover."

I do my small part... and the Lord does the healing!

A seventy-two year old lady in North Carolina came to me in her wheel chair for prayer. She had not even walked once in over five years. I anointed her with oil and prayed that Jesus would touch her. She slowly stood and began struggling across the front of the church. She continued to walk, back and forth, back and forth. By the tenth time, she was running, jumping, and shouting!

I will let her tell you the story in her own words:

> *"Since the revival, I have been changed forever. We were so blessed having you in our fellowship. Our Lord is a miracle working God!*
>
> *My body had been deteriorating for many years as a result of severe fybromyalgia. The Lord touched my body. I felt the strength come in. I had been completely confined to a wheel chair for more than five years. I was not even able to carry my Bible in church. I only attended church two or three times a month. I used a motor scooter in the stores.*
>
> *I had lost all sense of balance and was always concerned that I would fall. I no longer stagger or lose my balance. I ran a fever from intense pain. I had to lay down every few hours throughout the day. I was in bed at 7:00 every night. The pain was overwhelming. Doctors could only tell me it would get worse and I would be confined to a home for assisted living. Now I do not walk with a limp. All the pain is completely gone! To God be all the glory! My family rejoices with me! The song, **"He Touched Me"** now has new meaning for me!"*

Can you hear the words of the Great Physician as He announces in heaven, *"Case Dismissed"*?

Joe wrote from West Virginia:

> *"I attended your meeting this Spring. I asked for the*
> *handkerchief you preached with. I planned to give*
> *it to my friend who was dying of cancer. After much*
> *searching, you found it and gave it to me. It was too late*
> *to take it to him that night. My wife said, 'I wouldn't*
> *let that go to waste. I would put it on my heart if I were*
> *you!'*
>
> *I had a heart attack the previous year and had a very*
> *bad arrhythmia ever since. When my wife listened to it*
> *for the first time, she cried as she told me it sounded like*
> *an old engine sputtering and spurting and trying to quit!*
> *I slept with the handkerchief on my chest that night.*
> *My wife listened to my heart the next day and said it*
> *sounded perfect. I came to church and told everyone*
> *about it! When I returned to cardiac rehabilitation, the*
> *doctor said my heart was perfect. I went to my heart*
> *doctor for a stress test. The arrhythmia was gone. To*
> *God be all glory, honor, and praise!"*

Again we can almost see our heavenly Healer smiling as He says,
"Case Dismissed."

I have saved one of the most wonderful miracles of my brand new
life for last.

ANGIE

I FIRST MET ANGIE IN BIBLE COLLEGE, but it wasn't until I was addressing the pastors at a Minister's Retreat in her home church in West Monroe, Louisiana, that I recognized her in the audience.

She was as beautiful as I remembered. I looked at the elderly gentleman sitting next to her. He looked too old to be her husband or boyfriend. I learned after the service that he was definitely too old for Angie, who was twenty-three! She introduced me to her ninety-six year old grandfather, Reverend Ollie Livingston! I felt much more suited to her age at twenty-nine!

Angie and I began dating that night. Less than three months later, we were married. All who had known me during my life of sin and rebellion knew that I didn't deserve this pure, wonderful young lady who had lived for God her entire life. She had the greatest testimony a person can have—she had never strayed from her Savior. God in His great mercy blessed me with her.

I now had a dedicated wife to travel with me.

We were in a revival in Kailua, Hawaii, in October of 1995, when Angie dreamed that she gave birth to a stillborn daughter. Her voice was trembling as she shared her dream with me.

In her dream, a radio broadcast of James Dobson was playing in the background. He was interviewing an evangelist who said that people were being raised from the dead in his revival services. It was our daughter who was dead and needed a miracle. Angie dreamed that we called the evangelist, who instructed us to hold the lifeless body of our baby up in the air. As we all prayed, God miraculously breathed life into our baby. What a time of joy! This was a miracle! In her dream we named our little baby Miracle Joy.

The dream had a deep impact on Angie and remained with her. Six months after her dream when our son, Luke, was still a toddler, we learned that Angie was expecting twins! We were elated!

Our happiness turned to fear when Angie's doctor said he was alarmed because of Angie's dangerous symptoms. He sent us to one of the best Perinatologists in his field.

Extensive tests were performed, and we were told that one of the twins was at least two times larger than the other. Both were far too small for their gestational age. The smallest baby was stuck against the wall of Angie's womb.

The doctor tried to be compassionate. But how could he soften such a message of doom? Finally he just bluntly said: "Both twins will die." We were numb. It was all we could do to take in his words as he kept talking.

"At approximately twenty-four weeks, the smaller of the twins will pass away. Invariably, the process reverses, and within twenty-four hours, the larger twin will die of heart failure. The longest I have seen twins survive with this condition is twenty-eight weeks."

He told us the mortality rate for this condition was 95% to 100% for both twins.

We were stunned and barely heard the rest. "In addition to the Twin-to-Twin Transfusion syndrome, there is absolutely no amniotic fluid in the sacks of the twins to protect them while in the womb."

We had just been handed a death sentence, not for one daughter, but for two.

Doctor Neuman did not give us one word of hope.

"There is nothing I can do to correct the problem; no medication I can prescribe; no operation I can perform; no amount of rest or exercise Angie can do. All you can do is wait for what will inevitably end in death."

Then he added the words that jolted us out of our stupor: "It will take a miracle for either one of these twins to survive the pregnancy."

Angie sat up straight and looked Doctor Neuman directly in the eyes.

"Doctor Neuman, with all due respect, what you just said to us has gone in one ear and out the other."

She then pointed her finger at the ultrasound and said in a firm voice, "We have named this smallest twin Miracle Joy. We will walk out of this hospital with both babies—alive!"

I had just heard two voices and listened to two contrary messages.

One: **Death. Sorrow.**

The other: **Miracle. Joy.**

Every two weeks Angie's doctor monitored the progress of her pregnancy. And every two weeks, we were given more dark and hopeless news.

The twins were not growing.

They would both die.

Their condition is deteriorating.

We discovered the truth of Philippians 4:7: *"**And the peace of God, which passeth all understanding, shall keep your hearts and minds through Christ Jesus.**"*

The peace that passes all understanding...

Even we could not understand the perfect peace we had after hearing the most devastating news parents could hear.

Doctor Neuman repeated his prognosis time and time again, "Your twins will die."

We answered him with the Lord's report: "We will walk out of the hospital with both twins alive."

Dr. Neuman could say nothing to shatter our peace. The peace given to us by the Prince of Peace was beyond his understanding.

We not only had peace, we also had genuine joy and excitement. We **knew** God was going to give us our miracle.

I was sitting in my car praying one afternoon following another doctor's appointment. "God," I prayed. "You are a **now** God. **I claim healing** for our twins in Jesus' name."

The Holy Spirit filled the vehicle and spoke to my heart.

"Tim, are you through?"

"Yes, Lord."

"Tim, do you want to do this, or do you want **Me** to do this?"

I answered, "God, I want You to do this."

His voice was gentle. "Tim, I am accomplishing something bigger than what you can see."

OUR TINY TWINS

THROUGHOUT ANGIE'S ENTIRE PREGNANCY, there was not one medical factor that gave us even a shred of hope. At thirty-one weeks into her pregnancy, the situation was so bad that we made a decision to allow the doctors to take the twins by C-Section.

Mariah Faith weighed only two pounds and fourteen ounces. She was rushed to the Neonatal Intensive Care Unit. Within a week, she had stabilized. She remained hospitalized for seven weeks. Then we brought our precious daughter home.

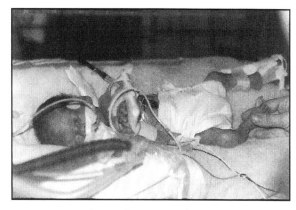

Mariah, weighing 2 pounds, 14 ounces

Miracle Joy, however, weighed only one pound and two ounces at birth. She joined her sister in the Neonatal Intensive Care Unit, where her weight dropped to twelve ounces. She was so tiny that I was able to fit my wedding band on her leg at the top of her thigh!

Her veins were so fragile that they began to fail within a week of her birth. There was no place remaining on her miniature body to insert an IV.

We held onto the promise of God as we watched her. Each minute she looked as if she could not possibly live another minute longer. The physicians had one more option. They ran a Central Line Placement through her little arm, into

Tim's wedding ring is on Miracle Joy's thigh. She weighs only 12 ounces.

the only threadlike vein that could accommodate it. The line was inserted through her chest and over to her heart.

"This is a standard procedure for a baby of normal size," the doctor explained. "For a twelve ounce baby, this is major surgery."

We were thrilled to hear that the procedure was a success.

Our telephone rang at 3:00 the next morning. The hospital staff physician, Dr. Voelker, explained that they had completely lost Miracle's heart rate and blood pressure. Her frail body had not responded to the medication they administered to stimulate her body.

She then tried to revive her by performing chest compressions, using only her thumbs to keep from crushing her tiny heart.

Dr. Voelker added, "Miracle is alive, but you may want to come to the hospital to be with her. She may not make it through the night."

Angie and I rushed to the hospital and gazed at our little Miracle. She did not look like a miracle. Tubes ran in and out of her nose, mouth, and navel. Tubes and needles were in her tiny arms and legs. Our little Miracle even had a wire coming out of the top of her head. Her skin had turned gray. Her stomach was bloated.

We were not looking at life.

We were looking at death.

I reached down to touch her. Doctor Voelker grabbed my wrist and stopped me with her words: "You cannot hold her! You cannot even touch her! The least bit of stimulation could cause her to go into cardiac arrest!"

We had been told we could not hold her until she was two and a half months old. I was her Daddy. With all my heart, I wanted to hold my daughter just once. It was all I could do to keep from lifting her in my arms and letting her feel my love for her as I held her close to me.

It was then that I heard the voice of another Daddy.

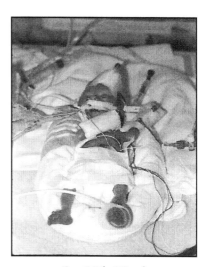

Our Little Miracle

"Tim, you are experiencing in a very small way what I went through when I had to leave my beloved Son hanging on the cross. I did not hold Him when He needed. I left Him there to save you."

MIRACLE! JOY!

THE TWINS WERE THREE WEEKS OLD when the prognosis from their doctors finally matched the news from our Great Physician.

"Both of your twins will live!"

Dr. Neuman wrote a letter stating that their birth was the most outstanding medical miracle he had seen in his entire practice! When I went to pick up a copy of his letter, his secretary said, "Brother Todd, I have worked for Dr. Neuman for more than twenty years. He has never allowed us to talk about God in this office. Now all he talks about is the miracle God performed on your twin girls!"

Her next words were the most exciting. "Dr. Neuman told me to tell you that if you read his letter in your home church, he will come to the service to listen to you." Then she added, "This is another Miracle. Dr. Neuman does not serve God nor does he attend church."

We made the arrangements to have his letter read on a Sunday morning. Dr. Neuman, his wife, and his four children were in the service.

After reading his letter, I went and sat with him as our Pastor, Jeff Ogg, ministered God's Word.

When Angie and I returned home, our phone was ringing.

Angie answered. Dr. Neuman had called to tell us that he had been raised in church as a young boy. When he went to medical school, he turned his back on God. He had not served God for over thirty years.

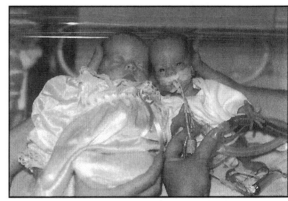

He said, "Your twin girls have had such an impact on my life. On our way home from church, my wife and I made a decision to get our priorities straight with the Lord. We are going to serve Him."

Very first picture of our twins together, taken on the day Mariah came home.

I remembered God's words that He had spoken weeks earlier. "Tim, I am accomplishing something bigger than what you can see."

I could hear the gavel slamming down above and the Lord's pleased voice saying, *"Case Dismissed. Forgiven."*

I was looking forward to bringing my beautiful twin daughters home.

As always, God was looking where my eyes could not see. He was looking forward to bringing His lost children home.

We were contacted by Dr. Neuman's mother.

"Thank you! Your twins were a witness to my son! He has never allowed me to talk to his children about the Lord. Now he wants me to talk to them about God all the time!"

God fulfilled His promise to us. We had our Miracle. We had our Joy!

We also had medical bills that exceeded a staggering half a million dollars!

Tim and Angie with Luke in the middle of his twin sisters.
(This photo appeared on the front page of the Baton Rouge
Advocate the day that Miracle came home.)

Dr. Neuman holding our beautiful twins.

BURIED IN DEBT

THE MEDICAL PROCEDURES HAD BEEN HUGE. We walked out of the hospital with Mariah Faith when she was seven weeks old. She had no medical problems.

We continued to hover over our little Miracle Joy in the hospital for nearly five months. It was a very slow and gradual process, but she finally began tolerating less than a teaspoonful of food each day through a tube. She breathed with the help of a ventilator for the first two and a half months of her life. Her frail body endured six major operations, each one a threat to end her life.

We finally walked out of the hospital with our little Miracle Joy. She had a heart monitor and a breathing monitor. Without her feeding tube implant, she could not eat. Without her oxygen, she could not breathe. She remained on oxygen for over a year.

We had a $65,000 insurance policy. It was used up in the first two days of our twins' lives! How could I pay these bills in a lifetime of work? I did not have a salary. I was working for the Lord ... Yes!

I was working for the LORD!

Was not my Employer the One who said, *"For every beast of the forest is mine, and the cattle upon a thousand hills. The silver is mine, and the gold is mine, saith the Lord of hosts"*? PSALM 50:10 AND HAGGAI 2:8

I was serving the same Jesus who told Peter to catch a fish to pay taxes they *did not owe!* Then He ordered a fish to pick up a coin and deliver it to where Peter stood fishing! Could not this Jesus provide over half a million dollars of medical bills that I *did owe?*

GOD, THE
MOUNTAIN MOVER

It was October 11 when I prayed specifically about my mountain of bills.

I was filled with faith. I expected a miracle! Instead I was given an unwelcome command.

God spoke to my heart: "Give $1,000 to a mission project."

I spoke back: "With all of these medical bills? I cannot afford to give $1,000 to missions right now!"

His voice was a demand.

"Tim, with all of your medical bills, you cannot afford not to give $1,000 to missions right now!"

I had expected to receive a check, not to be ordered to write one.

If I had learned one thing in my faith walk, it was my Savior's voice.

Jesus said, *"My sheep hear my voice, and I know them, and they follow me."* John 10:27

"My sheep hear my voice..." I had heard.

"...and they follow me." I followed.

I can't say I enjoyed writing that check, but I wrote it.

God had surely described Himself and me when He wrote: *"My thoughts are not your thoughts, neither are your ways my ways, saith the Lord. For as the heavens are higher than the earth, so are my ways higher than your ways, and my thoughts than your thoughts."* ISAIAH 55:8-9

My ways were to receive. His ways were to give.

Yet isn't that what Jesus commanded in LUKE 6:38? *"Give, and it shall be given unto you; good measure, pressed down, and shaken together, and running over, shall men give into your bosom."*

I knew that His ways are in direct opposition to the ways of men.

If we want to find new life, we must first lose our old one.

If we want to receive, we must first give!

I mailed the check that morning with a sigh.

After all, what was another $1,000 when I owed over $500,000?

The pile of bills was growing higher every day. I tried my best to avoid looking at it. I hated even getting my mail.

I leafed through the stack of bills that came the day I sent the $1,000 check to missions. In the middle of them was a letter from the director of the business office of the hospital. I reluctantly opened it, figuring it would be a demand for an immediate payment.

It was hard to even comprehend the Director's words as I read her letter.

She wrote, "*The Miracle Todd Twins* have been the talk of the hospital!"

She went on to explain that she had taken it upon herself to contact all of the medical carriers, the heart doctor, the lung doctor, the brain doctor, the pathologists, the hospital … and the list went on and on. Every single one of our creditors had unanimously agreed to write off their entire bill.

I was reeling. I owed nothing to no one.

I stared at the stack of bills. The Lord had just reduced them all to *…nothing! Zero!* What could have become a case had just been dismissed!

His promise was no longer just something to preach. It was an absolute Truth!

> *"Give, and it shall be given unto you; good measure, pressed down, and shaken together, and running over, shall men give into your bosom."*

I had given a paltry $1,000.

Men had given me over half a million dollars!

There was no doubt in my mind that this miracle was from my Lord.

PROVERBS 21:1 says, ***"The king's heart is in the hand of the Lord, as the rivers of water: he turneth it whithersoever he will."***

The One who has the power to turn the hearts of kings had turned the hearts of the medical personnel to give to us.

They had labored day and night, giving their time, facilities, and talents to save the lives of two tiny girls that they didn't even believe could live. They gave willingly and tirelessly— ***and took nothing.***

Tim and Angie with their 4 children — all two years old and under!

Another **Miracle.** More **Joy.**

Three days before our beautiful twins had their first birthday, sweet Mikalen Hope was born. We now had four children, two years old and younger.

The middle names of our three daughters are Faith, Joy, and Hope. God has turned my life of rebellion into one of faith. He has filled me with joy. Each new day brings hope as He continues to work in and through me.

I give all praise to JESUS, my merciful Savior and my eternal Lord.

> *"For this God is our God for ever and ever: he will be our guide even unto death."* Psalm 48:14

WHAT WILL YOU EXCHANGE FOR YOUR SOUL?

How my life has changed since I ran to the altar of the church that morning and met my Savior and my Lord.

I had walked away from Satan, the destroyer of my life—and had fallen into the arms of my Savior, Jesus Christ.

I left my life of sin and rebellion—and began my life of obedience to God.

Jesus replaced destruction with salvation and judgment with mercy.

While serving Satan, I was dodging bullets because I owed men $10,000.

While serving my Lord, my debt of over $500,000 was forgiven by my smiling creditors.

My feet were no longer walking toward hell—they are walking the path to eternal life.

My hands were no longer robbing and taking—they are offering Bread from the Master's table—love, forgiveness, and healing.

My mouth was no longer pouring out poison, filth, and curses—it is pouring out the life-giving Word of God.

My mind was no longer a cesspool of sin and confusion—it is filled with the peace that passes all understanding.

My trembling hand was no longer holding a loaded gun to my head — it is holding tightly to the nail-scarred hand of my Lord.

My heart was no longer shriveling with bitterness and anger. My Lord has filled it to overflowing with His love. I have a very good relationship with Mom, Dad, Linda, and Chuck. I have great respect and admiration for each one of them.

My older sisters, Janet and Gail, my older brother, Jon, and my younger brother, Cecil, have all survived the divorce. All of us, including my step-brother, Chuck, are in full-time ministry except for Jon, who faithfully serves God.

Dad is eighty years old as I write this. He is in good health and still preaches somewhere almost every weekend. He plans to preach until God takes him home! He founded Revival Fires® over sixty-two years ago. Then he passed the torch of the Revival Fires® Ministry to me in 2005 at one of his camp meetings. We moved its headquarters to West Monroe, Louisiana.

My reason for living is no longer for self-gain and glory. I want to please my Lord who has washed me in His own blood.

My friends are no longer people who shoot at me and offer me poison. My new friends offer me prayer, love, and encouragement.

I look at my beautiful, faithful wife, a very special woman of God who does not love sin, but loves her Savior with all her heart. She and my son, Luke, traveled the world with me until the twins were born. She has been my loving partner for twenty years.

I look at my wonderful seventeen year old son, Luke, who has been called into the ministry. He plays lead guitar in a youth worship band. Although we home school him, he goes with our youth pastor from our home church, John Skipworth, to the public school during lunch hour on Wednesdays to witness to the teens in high school.

I look at my perfectly healthy fifteen year old twin daughters, Mariah Faith and Miracle Joy, who are both alive and loving and serving the Lord.

I look at my sweet fourteen year old Mikalen, who has such a tender heart toward God. She is in choir and has a beautiful voice.

The Lord has used me for the past twenty-five years as a full time evangelist. My sole purpose is to introduce people to the merciful Savior who saved me from my dark life of sin.

Jesus alone has made me worthy to be Angie's faithful husband.

Jesus alone has molded me into a father who has raised his children to love and serve God with all their hearts, souls, minds, and strength.

Did I love my sin too much to exchange it for my Savior?

No! I love my life-giving Savior too much to exchange Him for sin and its destruction.

If you are still living as I did before Jesus saved me, turn to Him now. Don't wait until you are dodging bullets, lying in an ambulance, or holding a gun to your head. You may wait too late.

Just reach up to Jesus now with your hand of faith. He will lift you up and walk this life with you, right into His Father's arms. If you are reading this, you still have time to hear the slam of the gavel and the words of the Savior as He writes across your sins, *"Case Dismissed. Forgiven."*

If you are a parent, grandparent, son, daughter, aunt, uncle, brother, sister, or friend who has replaced hope for despair for your loved one's salvation, look at my life of rebellion, drugs, and destruction. Have faith! Jesus found me and saved me. Keep praying! Keep interceding!

If you have found Christ, but guilt is keeping you from serving the Lord, I want you to know that God specializes in making all things new. Can you be worse than the maniac who Jesus met in a cemetery, screaming, casting off his clothes, inhabited by thousands of devils, frightening people, and cutting himself? Please remember that after Jesus set him free, He used him to give his testimony!

Don't forget about the woman I already wrote about who had been married to five husbands and was living with her sixth man! He used her!

And He is using me. You have just read my story, and the B.C. *(Before Christ)* part of it was not good. God can not only save you —He wants to use you! Jesus treated me with mercy so He could use me to demonstrate His longsuffering to anyone who will believe on Him.

"Christ Jesus came into the world to save sinners: of whom I am chief. Howbeit for this cause I obtained mercy, that in me first Jesus Christ might shew forth all longsuffering, for a pattern to them which should hereafter believe on him to life everlasting." I TIMOTHY 1:15-16

If I can ever help you in any way, please call or write me.

The next few verses from Romans sum up my testimony and my prayer for you.

"Neither yield ye your members as instruments of unrighteousness unto sin: but yield yourselves unto God, as those that are alive from the dead, and your members as instruments of righteousness unto God.

"Know ye not, that to whom ye yield yourselves servants to obey, his servants ye are to whom ye obey; whether of sin unto death, or of obedience unto righteousness? Being then made free from sin, ye became the servants of righteousness.

" ...as ye have yielded your members servants to uncleanness and to iniquity unto iniquity; even so now yield your members servants to righteousness unto holiness. "For when ye were the servants of sin, ye were free from righteousness.

"What fruit had ye then in those things whereof ye are now ashamed? for the end of those things

is death. But now being made free from sin, and become servants to God, ye have your fruit unto holiness, and the end everlasting life.

"For the wages of sin is death; but the gift of God is eternal life through Jesus Christ our Lord."
ROMANS 6:13, 16, 18-23

ABOUT THE AUTHOR

Dr. Tim Todd, the President of Revival Fires® Ministries, Inc, has conducted evangelistic crusades across America and around the world in Russia, Latvia, India, Africa, the Bahama's, Mexico, Haiti and the Middle East.

Dr. Todd gathered and delivered one million signatures to then, House Speaker Newt Gingrich to restore voluntary prayer and Bible reading to America's public schools.

Dr. Todd has distributed in excess of 1.5 million "Truth for Youth" Bibles to America's public school students. The "Truth for Youth" was designed by

Dr. Todd and has been enthusiastically endorsed by some of America's most prominent spiritual leaders: Michael Reagan, T.D. Jakes, Rod Parsley, the late, Billy Joe Daugherty, the late, Jerry Falwell, Pat Boone, Actor Dean Jones, the late, Bill Bright, the late, Art Linkletter and Denny Duron.

Revival Fires® provided more than 150,000 Bibles for our troops during the Gulf War; more than 200,000 Bibles for our troops defending America in the war on terror in Afghanistan and Iraq; Five million Bibles for Russian military soldiers and young people in Russia's public schools; Revival Fires® built a Mercy Hospital, Nurses Training Center, 150 churches and two orphanages in Kerala State, India.

Dr. Todd attended Dallas Christian College in Dallas, TX, Central Bible College in Springfield, MO and has an earned Doctor of Theology from North Carolina College of Theology in Carolina Beach, North Carolina.

Dr. Todd resides in West Monroe, Louisiana with his precious wife, Angie and four children, Luke, Miracle, Mariah and Mikalen.

Revival Fires® Ministries
505 Good Hope Road
West Monroe, LA 71291

www.revivalfires.org
318.396.HOPE (4673)

REVIVAL FIRES INTERNATIONAL ORDER FORM

TIME IS RUNNING OUT!

MAY GOD FOREVER BLESS
Beautiful 16x20 full color picture depicting what happened on 9/11. For a donation of $100.00 or more to help us provide a case of Bibles for our armed forces defending America in the war on terror.

FIRST PRAYER IN CONGRESS
Commemorative 16x20 picture of the very 'First Prayer In Congress' along with picture history. For a donation of $100.00 or more to help us provide a case of **Truth for Youth** for young people in America's public schools.

TIME IS RUNNING OUT
16x20 full color picture of God holding an almost empty hour glass over the world facing toward America. For a donation of $100.00 or more to help us provide a case of Bibles for Russion Army soldiers.

Ministry Item	Quantity	Price (Includes shipping.)	How many?	Sub-total
The Truth For Youth Bible	1 Copy	$5.00 each		
The Truth For Youth Bible	2-49 Copies	$3.60 each		
The Truth For Youth Bible	50 or more	$2.50 each (at cost!)		
Hairy Polarity and the Sinister Sorcery Satire	1 Copy	$3.00 each		
Hairy Polarity and the Sinister Sorcery Satire	2-49 Copies	$2.00 each		
Hairy Polarity and the Sinister Sorcery Satire	50 or more	$1.25 each (below cost!)		
Case Dismissed! DVD	1	$15.00 each		
Freddy For Jesus! Children's Program DVD	1	$15.00 each		
America At The Crossroads DVD Album	1	$15.00 each		
Build Your House — 4 Message DVD Set	1	$30.00 each		
Kill A Lion In A Pit — 4 Message DVD Set	1	$30.00 each		
Four People I'd Like To See Go To Hell — 4 Message DVD Set	1	$30.00 each		
May God Forever Bless 9/11 Picture	1	$100.00 Gift to provide Bibles for US Troops		
First Prayer In Congress Picture	1	$100.00 Gift to provide TFY Bibles for teens		
Time Is Running Out Picture	1	$100.00 Gift to provide Bibles for Russia		
			Total:	$

☐ Check   ☐ Money Order   ☐ Visa   ☐ MasterCard   ☐ American Express   ☐ Discover

Name_____

Address_____

City _____ State____ Zip _____

Email_____

Card Number __ __ __ __ __ __ __ __ __ __ __ __ __ __ __ __

Expiration Date __ __ / __ __
(MM / YY)

CVV Code __ __ __ __ (Visa, MC, Discover: 3-Digits; American Express: 4-Digits)

TOTAL AMOUNT TO BE DEBITED: $

You may pay by credit card by calling **1.800.733.4737** or complete the above order form and send check, money order or credit card information to **Revival Fires International • PO Box 372 • West Monroe, LA 71294**
Make checks payable to Revival Fires International. All prices include shipping.
www.revivalfires.org • www.truthforyouth.com

Made in the USA
Charleston, SC
12 December 2012